Led by the Spirit

12 group study outlines from WordLive
Joel / Acts 1–4 / 1 Corinthians / Ephesians

Copyright © Scripture Union 2011
ISBN 978 1 84427 582 3
Scripture Union, 207–209 Queensway, Bletchley, MK2 2EB, England.
Email: info@scriptureunion.org.uk
Website: www.scriptureunion.org.uk

Scripture Union Australia, Locked Bag 2, Central Coast Business Centre,
NSW 2252 Australia
Website: www.scriptureunion.org.au

Scripture Union USA, PO Box 987, Valley Forge, PA 19482, USA
Website: www.scriptureunion.org

Scripture quotations taken from THE HOLY BIBLE, NEW INTERNATIONAL
VERSION®, NIV® Copyright © 1973, 1978, 1984, 2011 by Biblica, Inc.™
Used by permission. All rights reserved worldwide.

British Library Cataloguing-in-Data
A catalogue for this book is available from the British Library.

Cover and internal layout by Martin Lore

Contributors
Joel: Richard England
Acts 1–4: Phil Andrews
1 Corinthians: David Dewey; Dave Maclure; Andrew Clark; Emlyn Williams
Ephesians: Dave Maclure; Richard England
Extras: John Grayston, Annabel Robinson, Alan Hoare, Eric Gaudion, Gerard Kelly

Printed by Tien Wah Press, Singapore

Scripture Union is an international Christian charity working with churches in
more than 130 countries, providing resources to bring the good news about Jesus
to children, young people and families and encouraging them to develop spiritually
through the Bible and prayer.

Contents

Welcome to **God Moments Together**! This series provides you with straightforward Bible outlines which aim to help you meet with God as you get together with others to read the Bible and pray. It includes group material which first appeared on **wordlive.org**, Scripture Union's Bible reading website.

God Moments Together provides:

- Ready-to-use outlines wherever you meet – home, work, college, over a cup of coffee
- Flexibility and choice – variety of Bible books, series length
- Complementary resources available on *WordLive*
- A tear-off bookmark to help you read the Bible passages on your own

Led by the Spirit includes 12 group outlines from *WordLive* on Joel (1 session), Acts 1–4 (2 sessions), 1 Corinthians (6 sessions) and Ephesians (3 sessions). The theme explored aims to help us discover more about what it means to live in the power of the Holy Spirit.

Other titles in this series:
Meet Jesus: John's Gospel, Isaiah 6–10
The God Life: Matthew 1–11, James, 1 John, Genesis (Joseph)

How to use...

Each title in the **God Moments Together** series includes 12 or 13 session outlines on a Bible book or section of the Bible. Your group might decide to meet for several weeks as you read a complete Bible book, for example, a Gospel; or you might choose to meet for a couple of weeks to look, say, at the life of Joseph in Genesis. The timing of a session is up to you and your group – it can be as short or as long as you like.

The main heading tells you the Bible book and chapters on which the session's outline is based. It will help if everyone in the group has read these before you meet together – but don't worry if you don't manage to do this.

Get started is a simple icebreaker activity to start you talking and thinking about the session's theme.

Get stuck in aims to help you get into the Bible passages you've read. Talk together about what God might want to say to you through his Word.

Get real asks the 'So what?' questions. What does this mean for us? For me? What are we going to do about it? This section also provides some starting points for prayer for yourself and each other.

The second page of the outline includes several different elements:

A key Bible verse. If you remember nothing else, you could memorise this as your focus for the week.

Extras. In the first session of a series there will always be a brief introduction to the Bible book you are reading together. Other extras include helpful background information.

This week's readings gives a list of five daily readings which you might like to read during the week before you meet. Use the tear-off bookmark and keep it in your Bible.

Online resources gives a list of further resources for use with the session, which you can find at: **www.wordlive.org/ godmoments**

Notes is a space for you to write your own notes, thoughts and prayers as you share some God moments together each week.

Joel

Get started

Take five minutes to listen to a worship song such as 'The Spirit of God' (see **Online resources**), praying that God will lead you into his presence.

Get stuck in

Read **Joel 2:28–32** together.

- These verses are the best known in Joel, and are given great importance in the New Testament (see Acts 2). What strikes you as you read them?

- Verses 28 and 29 describe a new chapter in God's relationship with his people. How does Joel's vision mark a departure from much of the Old Testament in the way God works among his people?

- Previously, the Holy Spirit had only been given to a select few. In Joel's vision, many cultural barriers are broken down – young and old, male and female, slave and free – so that 'all people' can receive. What experiences have you had of the Spirit being poured out?

- Here, the evidence of the gift of the Spirit is prophecy. This echoes Moses' desire in Numbers 11:29 and is reflected in Paul's teaching in 1 Corinthians 14:31. What is prophecy for, and what experiences have you had of it?

- 'Intimate communication' is a hallmark of the Spirit. When was the last time you felt God speaking to you? Is it something that happens regularly?

Get real

Hearing God's voice is a privilege of being children of God. But learning to listen takes time and practice. Spend some time in quiet, listening to the Lord. Share anything you hear. Pray for each other that hearing God's voice would become easier in the week ahead.

> **'And afterwards, I will pour out my Spirit on all people. Your sons and daughters will prophesy, your old men will dream dreams, your young men will see visions. Even on my servants, both men and women, I will pour out my Spirit in those days.'**
>
> Joel 2:28,29

Introduction to Joel

We know nothing about the prophet Joel beyond the short description he gives us of himself in 1:1. It is generally thought that he was one of the earliest of all the Old Testament prophets, and he might well have known both Elijah and Elisha in his youth. He prophesied in the southern kingdom, Judah, perhaps during the reign of Joash (2 Kings 11,12).

The key phrase in Joel is 'the day of the Lord'. The country had recently been devastated by a plague of locusts, and for Joel this had a spiritual significance. He believed that the locusts had been a divine judgement, God's response to the people's sin. But greater judgement was at hand: Judah was surrounded by hostile nations like hordes of locusts. Their only hope lay in repentance.

Nevertheless, Joel was a prophet of hope. In fact he has been called 'the prophet of religious revival' (see 2:18–32). We can see this particularly in the events of the day of Pentecost when some of Joel's prophecies were fulfilled. Of course some still await fulfilment (2:28,29; Acts 2:16–21).

This week's readings

- Joel 1:1–12
- Joel 1:13–20
- Joel 2:1–11
- Joel 2:12–27
- Joel 2:28–32

Online resources

To enhance your session, go to **www.wordlive.org/godmoments** for these multimedia resources:

- Visual meditation: 'God's gift'
- Worship song: 'The Spirit of God'
- Vox pops video: 'Are you ready for the end of the world?'
- Audio Bible readings

Notes

Spirit-filled

Acts 1,2

Get started

If possible, listen worshipfully to 'The Spirit of God' – a song that describes the role of the Spirit in God's purposes and our lives (see **Online resources**). Alternatively, share with each other your understanding of the role of the Holy Spirit.

Get stuck in

Read **Acts 2:1–21** together.

- Churches vary a great deal in their thinking about the activity of the Holy Spirit in the lives of Christians today. Spend some time discussing what your church believes, comparing it to what this passage suggests about the role of the Spirit among believers 'in the last days' (v 17).

- Among Jesus' final words to his disciples was the instruction, 'Do not leave Jerusalem, but wait for the gift my Father promised …' (Acts 1:4,5). Why was it so important that they received the Holy Spirit before they embarked on the great commission (see Matthew 28:19,20)?

- The impact of the Holy Spirit on the believers was instant and public (vs 5–11). What does it tell us about the inclusiveness of the gospel that people from such diverse places who had gathered in Jerusalem for Pentecost could hear and understand what was said about 'the wonders of God' in their own languages (v 11)?

- As a group, compile a list of the different ways the Holy Spirit works in us according to Scripture (see particularly John 14:16–19; 15:26,27; 16:7–15; 1 Corinthians 12:1–11). In what ways do we demonstrate the presence of the Holy Spirit in our lives (v 17)?

Get real

If you can, listen to the 'Wind and fire' meditation (see **Online resources**). Alternatively, spend time as a group inviting the Holy Spirit to fill each person anew with his presence and power to live for the glory of Jesus.

'All of them were filled with the Holy Spirit and began to speak in other tongues as the Spirit enabled them.'

Acts 2:4

Introduction to Acts

Luke, the only non-Jewish writer in the New Testament, wrote Acts as a sequel to his earlier volume, the Gospel bearing his name. The first 12 chapters deal mostly with the activities of the apostle Peter, whilst the remaining chapters are taken up largely with the work of the apostle Paul.

Jesus had told his disciples that when the Holy Spirit had come upon them, they would be his witnesses. The book of Acts shows how this came to pass. From the book of Acts we learn a good deal about the early church, its joys and sorrows, its triumphs and tragedies, but above all its expansion so that in a few short years it was established throughout the civilised world.

We know Luke to have been a very careful historian and we can be assured that here we have a factual account of the early days of Christianity. Almost certainly Luke wrote Acts in the early or mid-sixties of the first century – at the close of Paul's two-year imprisonment in Rome. It covers the period from the founding of the church in Jerusalem to Paul's imprisonment in Rome – some thirty years.

Online resources

To enhance your session, go to **www.wordlive.org/godmoments** for these multimedia resources:

- Worship song: 'The Spirit of God'
- Audio meditation: 'Wind and fire'
- Audio: 'Speaking in tongues'
- Audio Bible readings

This week's readings

- Acts 1:1–11
- Acts 1:12–26
- Acts 2:1–13
- Acts 2:14–39
- Acts 2:40–47

Extra info

Prior to the events in Acts, Pentecost was a Jewish harvest festival, also known as the Feast of Weeks. It was celebrated 50 days after Passover to commemorate the giving of the Law to Moses. After the coming of the Spirit, Pentecost became a significant Christian festival, celebrating the birth of the church, and is always 50 days after Easter.

Notes

Acts 3:1 – 4:31

Get started

Discuss in twos or threes your experiences of talking about Jesus to non-Christians in any context. How did your audience respond? Were they interested, negative, confused? How did their reaction make you feel?

Get stuck in

Read **Acts 4:1–31** together.

- Talk about the purpose of divine healing in the passage, in the church today and within wider society. Is it simply to make people well or does it have a greater value in God's purposes (vs 8–10)?

- Do you think Peter's behaviour towards the Sanhedrin was disrespectful or justified? What does it teach us about how Christians should relate to the rules of their society and those who make them (vs 18–20)?

- How might the truth about Jesus' death and resurrection challenge the authority of those who govern, in this passage and in our day? Where do you see Christian values reflected in the workings of your government?

- Is it possible for us to be as fearless as the first believers were in telling people the truth about Jesus? What is the effect of proclamation being accompanied by miracles (vs 29,30), and how can churches today follow this model?

- Look again at the believers' prayer in verses 24–30. What impresses you about their response to persecution? Would you be willing to accept persecution with boldness for the advancement of God's kingdom?

Get real

Find some accounts of Christians who are being persecuted for their faith (try www.opendoorsuk.org for some powerful stories) and pray together that those who are being persecuted will be 'filled with the Holy Spirit and speak the word of God boldly' (see v 31). Then, pray the same thing for yourselves.

'And they were all filled with the Holy Spirit and spoke the word of God boldly.'

Acts 4:31b

The Sanhedrin

The council in Jerusalem, the Sanhedrin, had its roots in the period after the return from exile, although the concept probably goes back to the elders whom Moses appointed (Exodus 18:17–27).

The extent of its powers varied. Under Herod the Great (40–4 BC) its powers were limited, but they increased under the rule of the Roman Procurators from AD 6, although they seem to have been limited to Judea. It was abolished in AD 70 after the fall of Jerusalem.

One document suggests that there were 71 members. In the centuries before Jesus it was made up largely from the priestly aristocracy, mainly Sadducees, but from about 70 BC a larger number of Pharisees were included. This led to tensions (Acts 23:6–10).

This week's readings

- Acts 3:1–10
- Acts 3:11–26
- Acts 4:1–12
- Acts 4:13–22
- Acts 4:23–31

Online resources

To enhance your session, go to **www.wordlive.org/ godmoments** for these multimedia resources:

- Vox pops video: 'How do you tell others about Jesus?'
- Visual prayer: 'How to use power and influence people...'
- Audio: 'The believers' psalm'
- Audio Bible readings

Notes

Amos Obadiah Jonah Miach Nahum Habakkuk Zephaniah Haggai Zechariah Malachi Matthew Mark Luke John **Acts** Romans 1 Corinthians

1 Corinthians 1–3

Get started

Invite group members to list what they would look for in their 'ideal church' (being careful not to end up listing what you dislike about your church as it is!).

Get stuck in

Read **1 Corinthians 3:10,11** together.

- The church's one foundation is Jesus Christ. In what ways do you think today's churches are being faithful or unfaithful to Christ?

- Recently, church divisions have been highlighted in the press, most notably over gay clergy and the blessing of same-sex relationships. Are they the most important issues? What advice can be taken from these chapters?

Read **1 Corinthians 1:10 – 2:5** together.

- How can the cult of celebrity that seems to exist in some Christian circles today be remedied?

- Look at 1 Corinthians 1:30, noticing its context in Paul's comments about wisdom and what is worth boasting about (vs 26–31). What does it actually mean to call Christ our wisdom, righteousness, holiness and redemption?

- How could your church be more cross-centred than it is?

- Reflecting on these chapters, what do you think are the essential elements of Christian unity? Is obedience to the command 'Love one another' sufficient expression of our unity, or is more than love needed, eg a clear statement of faith?

Get real

List the activities of your church, then spend some time praying that these activities will bear 'fruit that will last'.

Or look together at the 'Build with care' animation (see **Online resources**) and reflect on whether you are growing to maturity in Christ.

'For no one can lay any foundation other than the one already laid, which is Jesus Christ.'

1 Corinthians 3:11

Introduction to 1 Corinthians

Corinth was a major city in ancient Greece. Strategically situated at the end of the narrow strip of land between the Aegean Sea and the Gulf of Corinth, it controlled the shipping routes east and west.

It flourished in classical Greece as a centre of trade, manufacturing, artistic creativity, healing and religion. It had been razed to the ground by the Roman army in 146 BC and lay in ruins for a century until Julius Caesar ordered that it be rebuilt as a Roman colony.

Paul had spent over a year at Corinth, preaching and teaching, and supporting himself by tentmaking (see Acts 18:1–17). Eventually he left for Ephesus and Jerusalem. In his absence, Apollos continued his work (see Acts 18:18–28).

Online resources

To enhance your session, go to **www.wordlive.org/ godmoments** for these multimedia resources:

- Animation: 'Build with care'
- Audio poem: 'The wisdom of God'
- Visual prayer: 'Keep giving thanks'
- Audio Bible readings

Notes

This week's readings

- 1 Corinthians 1:1–9
- 1 Corinthians 1:10–17
- 1 Corinthians 1:18 – 2:5
- 1 Corinthians 2:6–16
- 1 Corinthians 3:1–23

Extra info

The Greek word for 'spiritual gift' is *charisma*, which is derived from *charis*, meaning 'grace'. Spiritual gifts are God's free gifts to the church. There are three places in the New Testament which discuss specific spiritual gifts:

- Romans 12:6–8
- 1 Corinthians 12:7–11
- Ephesians 4:11–13

The lists are different in each place, which suggests that there is not a fixed list of spiritual gifts, as some claim, but rather that God equips each congregation with the gifts that it needs.

1 Corinthians 4:1 – 7:16

Staying faithful

Get started

Imagine your church has the chance to employ the perfect pastor from any time in history. Ask the group who they would choose and why. You may want to prompt the group by suggesting a few names, such as Martin Luther, Billy Graham or Philip Yancey.

Get stuck in

Read **1 Corinthians 4,5** together.

- How does your job description of a perfect pastor match up with 1 Corinthians 4?

- How does Paul's description of the cost of church leadership (4:9–13) fit with contemporary understandings of leadership – both inside and outside of the church?

- Is there ever a place for barring people from fellowship as a means of maintaining church discipline (see 5:9–13)? Under what circumstances would this be acceptable? And with what conditions attached?

Read **1 Corinthians 6:1 – 7:16** together.

- How far do you think Christians should go in standing up for their individual rights – both inside and outside of the church building (see 6:1–11)?

- Without putting anyone on the spot, ask for suggestions of how Christians can apply the teaching contained in 1 Corinthians 6:12 – 7:16. You may like to listen to the comedy sketch, 'Sex and the kingdom', first (see **Online resources**).

Get real

In advance of the group meeting, contact one or more of your church leaders. Ask what prayer requests they have, and commit yourself to praying regularly for them. If they are present at your meeting, you might like to gather round them as a group and pray over them.

'Do you not know that your bodies are temples of the Holy Spirit, who is in you, whom you have received from God? You are not your own; you were bought at a price.'

1 Corinthians 6:19,20a

5

Marriage guidance

Many of the believers in Corinth were Gentiles, and did not have the high view that orthodox Jews placed on marriage.

- The Scriptures show marriage to be a God-given environment for a man and a woman to experience oneness.

- Paul will teach elsewhere that marriage is the mysterious replica of the intimate relationship Christ has with his bride, the church (see Ephesians 5:32).

- The culture of today must never be allowed to dictate to or diminish this holy institution.

Some of the new Christians in Corinth were over-emphasising the cause of Christ to the detriment of their marriages. There was pressure to abandon the restrictions of marriage in order to be free to serve the Lord. Paul firmly corrected this view. Our faith must enhance, not destroy our marriages. Marriage is the primary relationship where faith and love are worked out.

This week's readings

- 1 Corinthians 4:1–21
- 1 Corinthians 5:1–13
- 1 Corinthians 6:1–11
- 1 Corinthians 6:12–20
- 1 Corinthians 7:1–16

Online resources

To enhance your session, go to **www.wordlive.org/godmoments** for these multimedia resources:

- Vox pops video: 'Punishment'
- Audio drama: 'Bad judge of character'
- Audio drama: 'Sex and the kingdom'
- Audio Bible readings

Notes

1 Corinthians 7:17 – 9:27

Get started

Imagine your group is a church leadership team – involved in the running of the church, setting its vision, caring for the pastoral needs of church members and dealing with any issues that arise. Using this week's Bible passages, how would you respond to each of the following scenarios?

Get stuck in

- Lucy, living with a partner, starts attending your church and becomes a Christian. She wants to be baptised. What is the group's response? How can Lucy best be supported (see 1 Corinthians 7:17–24)?

- After a while Lucy wants to get married, but her unbelieving partner, Dave, doesn't think that it's necessary. What advice should you give them? Should she stay with him? If they have children, does this make a difference (see 7:25–31,36–40)?

- Later again, Lucy – still unmarried, but now a strong Christian – wants to be involved in the children's work of the church. How should your team respond? Remember that you will need to offer grace and encouragement, while being mindful that some parents may be critical (see 7:32–35)?

- Steve, a committed member of the church, invites the whole congregation to his 40th birthday party. Gary and Jackie, two recovering alcoholics on the fringes of faith, plan to attend. Should everyone be only offered soft drinks at Steve's party or should something be said to the couple beforehand (see 8:7–13)?

- John – inexperienced and from a very sheltered background – feels called to full-time Christian service. He comes to you for advice – what should you say to him (see 9:1–18)?

Get real

We need the wisdom of Solomon – and the help of God's loving Spirit! Pray for anyone in your group or church in similar situations to those above, and for your church leaders.

'Run in such a way as to get the prize ...a crown that will last for ever.'

1 Corinthians 9:24,25

Was Paul anti-women?

It is often argued that Paul was anti-women. He certainly seems proud to be single (7:7)! The argument is supported by his words about women being under authority (11:1–16) and keeping silent in church (14:33–35), along with 1 Timothy 2:11–15.

But these are difficult texts to interpret, and whatever Paul intends to prohibit in chapter 14 it is not praying or prophesying, which he regards as proper activities for women in 11:5. Questions about the nature of authority and the way it is to be exercised add to the difficulty.

But this chapter hardly supports such a view. Marriage – and sex within marriage (vs 1–6) – is a God-given good. He sees women as having equal status with men (see Galatians 3:28) and values their ministry (eg Romans 16:1,3,6,7,12,15).

We cannot conclude that Paul was against women or even against women in ministry, for he affirms their contribution. He does, on the other hand, have concerns that the gospel is not brought into disrepute and is anxious that both men and women behave in appropriate ways.

This week's readings

- 1 Corinthians 7:17–24
- 1 Corinthians 7:25–40
- 1 Corinthians 8:1–13
- 1 Corinthians 9:1–18
- 1 Corinthians 9:19–27

Online resources

To enhance your session, go to **www.wordlive.org/ godmoments** for these multimedia resources:

- Audio: 'Eat the meat?'
- Visual meditation: 'Compete for the crown'
- Audio drama: 'Finishing the race'
- Audio Bible readings

Notes

1 Corinthians 10:1 – 11:34

Get started

Think of a time you ignored a warning from someone – what were the consequences? Or think of a time you heeded a warning – did the warning save you from danger in some way?

Get stuck in

Read **1 Corinthians 10:7–13** together.

- What does the passage teach us about complacency in our decisions as Christians?

Read **1 Corinthians 10:18–22** together.

- What do we learn about the nature of our devotion to Christ from this passage? What principles can we apply to our lifestyles more widely?

Read **1 Corinthians 10:23,24,31** together.

- What influence does your concern for the 'good of others' have upon your behaviour? How much does living for the 'glory of God' mean the same thing?

Read **1 Corinthians 11:2–16** together.

- Read 'The politics of hair' together (see **Online resources**). Talk about what messages your church is giving out about what it means to be a Christian in your culture today.

Read **1 Corinthians 11:27–32** together.

- In what ways might we approach communion in an 'unworthy manner'? What is 'a worthy approach'?

Get real

Pray for one another to live in such a way that we work both for the good of others and the glory of God. If appropriate, you could end your time together by sharing some wine (or a non-alcoholic alternative) and bread to symbolise the unity you have in Christ.

'So whether you eat or drink or whatever you do, do it all for the glory of God.'

1 Corinthians 10:31

Social problems at Corinth

Some of Corinth's ethical and social problems may shock us. We need to remember that this multi-ethnic congregation comprised a spectrum of Christians from the very wealthy to slaves.

They had no role models to show them how to live as a congregation. The lives they knew outside the church kept strict social segregation between Jew and Gentile, masters and slaves, citizens and immigrants. The roles of men and women were socially prescribed.

The church met in people's homes. Their houses would have preserved such segregation, with women's quarters, men's quarters, slave quarters. So it is not surprising that when they met at homes for worship, some came as guests, and ate well (some even getting drunk); some came as slaves and were expected to keep their place. The poor came hungry.

They had yet to learn how to live and worship as 'one in Christ Jesus'. They had to lay aside their natural preoccupation with status. The slave would learn dignity, the master humility. They had never known anything like it before.

Online resources

To enhance your session, go to **www.wordlive.org/godmoments** for these multimedia resources:

- Audio poem: 'The footfall of faith'
- Visual prayer: 'Walk his way'
- PDF: 'The politics of hair'
- Audio Bible readings

This week's readings

- ■ 1 Corinthians 10:1–13
- ■ 1 Corinthians 10:14–22
- ■ 1 Corinthians 10:23 – 11:1
- ■ 1 Corinthians 11:2–16
- ■ 1 Corinthians 11:17–34

Extra info

People often think of idolatry as materialism. But that doesn't quite capture the sin that makes God so angry. God created the material world and means for us to enjoy it (see 1 Timothy 6:17). Idolatry creeps in when we turn to material things to do for us what only God can do – fulfil our longings, give meaning to our lives, and fulfil our need for relationships.

Notes

Gifts of the Spirit

1 Corinthians 12:1 – 14:25

Get started

Explain to the group that, together, they are responsible for completing a task. The rule is that every member must contribute to it in some way, but each contribution must be different. So, for example, only one member can give encouragement, only one member can use their hands, and so on.

Suggested tasks: put seven books into a neat pile; move a chair from one side of the room to the other.

Get stuck in

Read **1 Corinthians 12:1–11** together.

- What is your immediate reaction when you hear the term 'spiritual gifts'? Why do you think that is?

- The Corinthians would have been used to 'spiritual experiences' from their pagan days (v 2). These days lots of people are interested in spirituality. Do you think this is helpful or unhelpful in terms of experiencing the gifts of the Holy Spirit?

- The whole Godhead (Spirit, Son and Father) is involved in the giving of these gifts (vs 4–6). Talk about what you think about the nature and purpose of spiritual gifts in the church.

- What are three key things about spiritual gifts mentioned in verses 7 and 11? What is another key thing that Paul emphasises in the practice of spiritual gifts (14:1)?

- How would you define each gift mentioned in the passage? Are these gifts particularly special, or are others just as important (see Romans 12:6–8; Ephesians 4:11–13)?

Get real

Encourage the group to be quiet in God's presence, and ask him to speak to them. Then suggest that they respond to the Spirit's prompting – you might share a Bible verse, say something else you feel God is leading you to share, or ask for prayer for your own or someone else's healing.

> 'Now to each one the manifestation of the Spirit is given for the common good ... All these are the work of one and the same Spirit, and he distributes them to each one, just as he determines.'

1 Corinthians 12:7,11

8

Spiritual gifts

Gifts of the Spirit are also listed in Romans 12:6–8 and Ephesians 4:11–13.

Spiritual gifts are:

- Empowered by the Holy Spirit
- For the common good of the church
- For the building up of God's people

This week's readings

- ▉ 1 Corinthians 12:1–11
- ▉ 1 Corinthians 12:12–31a
- ▉ 1 Corinthians 12:31b – 13:13
- ▉ 1 Corinthians 14:1–12
- ▉ 1 Corinthians 14:13–25

Online resources

To enhance your session, go to **www.wordlive.org/ godmoments** for these multimedia resources:

- Vox pops video: 'Love'
- Interactive animation: 'Pray for church ministries'
- Interactive animation: 'Building with gifts'
- Audio Bible readings

Notes

1 Corinthians 14:26 – 16:24

Get started

Being sensitive to the different experiences of the group, ask people to share their experiences of attending funerals, particularly their memories of what was said in the services. What messages were conveyed about the future of those who had died?

Get stuck in

Read **1 Corinthians 15:12–34** together.

■ How do the things you have heard at funerals match up to the teaching of this passage?

■ Why is Christ's resurrection so important? What would be the implications if the story of the resurrection was untrue?

■ Does Paul's teaching in this passage challenge any notions you have about the future? How?

■ What does Paul have to say here about those who have already died?

■ How would this passage help you when talking to someone who had just experienced the death of a friend or relative? Would it create any problems for you?

■ What are the implications of this teaching for the way you live your life?

Get real

Use this passage as a stimulus to pray for those who are suffering from the death of friends or relatives. These could be:

■ people known to the group who have been bereaved
■ families and friends of those whose funerals have been held in your church
■ people connected to deaths you have read about in local and national newspapers

'But thanks be to God! He gives us the victory through our Lord Jesus Christ.'

1 Corinthians 15:57

9

Facing the end

Death is a great puzzle and a great fear. It is the end of all that is familiar, and what lies beyond is unknown. It may well involve physical and emotional pain. It may mean distressing farewells. So it is hardly surprising that we shrink from it.

Paul's assurance that death has lost its power and has no hold on us may not take away all the questions and will certainly not remove all the pain or distress. But it reminds us that it is not the end but the beginning. It opens the way to the full enjoyment of a life that is more intense and offers greater satisfaction than the life of this age.

Christians can therefore approach death with a different set of attitudes. Because we look forward to something better, we can offer hope in a world that fears death. We need to be sensitive in our approach, but we can tell people that there is bigger picture, that Jesus has removed the sting of death and that if we will put our trust in him we can pass through it into life eternal.

This week's readings

- 1 Corinthians 14:26–40
- 1 Corinthians 15:1–11
- 1 Corinthians 15:12–34
- 1 Corinthians 15:35–58
- 1 Corinthians 16:1–24

Online resources

To enhance your session, go to **www.wordlive.org/ godmoments** for these multimedia resources:

- Image: 'In the twinkling of an eye…'
- Visual meditation: 'Pass it on…'
- Visual meditation: 'Together we are strong'
- Audio Bible readings

Notes

The riches of his grace

Ephesians 1:1 – 3:13

Get started

Describe a present you received unexpectedly – when it wasn't even your birthday or Christmas.

Get stuck in

Read **Ephesians 2:1–10** together.

- Paul begins chapter 2 making a comparison: 'As for you…' Briefly look back at the last few verses of chapter 1. What is the first half of the comparison and what point is Paul making about the power that Jesus wields?

- Who or what is 'the ruler of the kingdom of the air' (2:2) and should we be aware of him/it in our day?

- Paul says before Christ we were 'objects of wrath'. Why does Paul use such strong language to describe the spiritual state of people who don't know Jesus? Are there situations you can think of where it would be right for us to speak so strongly?

- 'If God does everything to bring us salvation then I can just sit back, relax and watch God save me and the people around me – anyway, there's nothing I can do to change his mind.' This is one possible response to the verses on grace and works (vs 8–10) – but was this the reaction Paul intended (see Romans 6:15–23)?

- When Paul speaks of the 'coming ages' he is talking about the church, which includes us today, 2,000 years later. How has God shown the 'incomparable riches of his grace' in your church and in your own life?

- What assurance can you take from verses 6–10 for how you live today and for your eternal future?

Get real

Spend some time in prayer and praise before God. First, pray for forgiveness and thank God that he chose to have mercy on us 'objects of wrath'. Secondly, praise God for the promises of his Word, his grace to us and the hope we have.

> **'For it is by grace you have been saved, through faith – and this is not from yourselves, it is the gift of God.'**
>
> Ephesians 2:8

Introduction to Ephesians

Loving others is not an optional extra for Christians, something Many people think this letter was intended for a wider circulation than the actual church at Ephesus. It was probably a sort of circular letter written for common use among different Christian groups in the neighbourhood of Ephesus. What Paul has to say in this letter is applicable to God's people generally and is not addressed to one particular church.

The letter was written like the epistles of Philippi and Colossae from a prison cell and it has for its main theme the nature, character and destiny of the Christian church – 'God's new society' as it has been called. The letter deals with no particular problems but its purpose it to exalt the name of Jesus Christ and to point to the importance of the Christian church as God's instrument in the world.

This week's readings

- Ephesians 1:1–14
- Ephesians 1:15–23
- Ephesians 2:1–10
- Ephesians 2:11–22
- Ephesians 3:1–13

Online resources

To enhance your session, go to **www.wordlive.org/ godmoments** for these multimedia resources:

- Visual meditation: 'Name it and claim it?'
- Vox pops video: 'Why pray?'
- Audio Bible readings

Notes

Ephesians 3:14 – 4:32

Get started

Use a *Guinness World Records* book (or go to www. guinnessworldrecords.com) and find a section that describes the largest or biggest things on earth. Choose someone to read out some of the items listed (eg 'World's largest hotel room') and ask the rest of the group to try and guess the dimensions involved (2 km long!). Award points for those who get closest to the real answers.

Get stuck in

Read **Ephesians 3:14–21** together.

- Reread verses 14, 15 and 21. How do these opening and closing comments shape our vision of our position and status in God's family?

- Paul asks us 'to know' something that surpasses 'knowledge' (v 19). How is the love of Christ something we can experience fully but not understand totally?

- Paul talks about love at various parts in his prayer – is it always the same thing? What is Paul's message concerning love for believers like us?

- Consider the line in Paul's prayer, 'to him who is able to do immeasurably more than all we ask or imagine'. Are we limited in what we ask of or expect from God? How might an increase in your expectation change the way you pray?

- Is this prayer anything like your prayers? What can we apply from Paul's techniques?

Get real

Using sentences from Paul's prayer to begin your own prayers, lift up to God other Christians you know who need some greater encouragement. To finish, stand together and read Paul's prayer aloud together as a group. Personalise the prayer by rephrasing it (eg changing 'I' for 'we' etc) to direct it at one another.

'I pray that out of his glorious riches he may strengthen you with power through his Spirit in your inner being...'

Ephesians 3:16

11

Just imagine

What place does imagination have in prayer? Paul seems to imply here a chain of events. We imagine what might be, we ask for it, and God surpasses even our wildest dreams.

But what if we struggle even to imagine? What if we look at the world we live in and cannot even picture it changing? Might we need a revolution in the realm of our dreams?

As American missiologist Dan Davis puts it, 'If God can do more than we can ask or imagine, why not ask for more imagination?'

Imagine a world transformed by God's grace; ask for the changes you have begun to imagine; and stand amazed at what God can do. Is your prayer life made poorer by the poverty of your dreams?

This week's readings

- Ephesians 3:14–21
- Ephesians 4:1–6
- Ephesians 4:7–16
- Ephesians 4:17–24
- Ephesians 4:25–32

Online resources

To enhance your session, go to **www.wordlive.org/ godmoments** for these multimedia resources:

- Vox pops video: 'Unconditional love'
- Worship song: 'Your love'
- Audio Bible readings

Notes

Ephesians 5,6

Get started

If possible, begin by playing 'I need a holiday' by Scouting for Girls. Then, share your best or worst experiences of work. Or, you could use a clip from a DVD (eg *The Office*) to prompt thoughts about the workplace or just talk about your experiences.

Get stuck in

Read **Ephesians 6:1–9** together.

- Paul's vision of following Jesus encompasses all of life, particularly our relationships. How might his instructions for family life in verses 1–4 be at odds with the way many families work?

- These days, the idea that Paul accepts slavery is hard for us to understand. Why doesn't he simply denounce it?

- As followers of Jesus, our attitude to work will be subtly changed. In verses 5–8, how does Paul suggest slaves should change their attitudes to their work? Why?

- Many Christians find it difficult to integrate their faith and their work. If we changed 'slaves' to 'employees', what attitudes might God challenge us to have towards our work?

- In its context, verse 9 is a bombshell. Paul challenges slave-owners to act toward their slaves as they'd want their slaves to act towards them. In which ways might God challenge employers today?

- If we tried to put these values into practice (wherever our workplaces are: home, employment or education), what practical changes might we need to make?

Get real

Share one change you need to make in your attitude to work, so that you can work 'as if you were serving the Lord, not people' (v 7). What practical thing could you do to help? Pray for each other as you make plans, and keep each other accountable in the weeks ahead.

'Serve wholeheartedly, as if you were serving the Lord, not people.'

Ephesians 6:7

12

Radical relationships

In Greco-Roman society, a father not only had the responsibility to raise his children: he had the power of life and death over them. Their lives were not their own. So too the slave-owner, who could call for the punishment or even execution of his 'property' with great ease and with scant regard for justice.

Thus Paul's injunction to children to obey their parents (v 1) and slaves to serve their masters well (v 5) would cause hardly a ripple in the gossip pond of Ephesus. But a call to fathers not to exasperate their children (v 4)? And a challenge to slave-owners to treat their slaves in the same way they expect to be treated by them (v 9)? These are the makings of a revolution.

The essence of the teaching is this: if you are the one who has power in the relationship, be willing to give it up for the sake of love. And if you are powerless – as women, children and slaves predominantly were in Paul's day – then choose to serve (v 5) rather then being forced to; serve God in them (v 7).

This week's readings

■ Ephesians 5:1–20
■ Ephesians 5:21–33
■ Ephesians 6:1–9
■ Ephesians 6:10–17
■ Ephesians 6:18–24

Online resources

To enhance your session, go to **www.wordlive.org/ godmoments** for these multimedia resources:

■ Video: 'Dave cam'
■ Video: 'An understanding of submission'
■ Vox pops video: 'Wives submit!'
■ Audio Bible readings

Notes

Here are some other resources from Scripture Union to help you keep on reading the Bible regularly – in your small group and individually:

Group material

The **Multi-Sensory** series: popular resources for creative small groups, youth groups and churches that appeal to a wide range of learning styles:

Sue Wallace, *Multi-Sensory Prayer*, Scripture Union, 2000
Sue Wallace, *Multi-Sensory Scripture*, Scripture Union, 2005

The **LifeBuilder** series: small group study material. Many titles including topical and character studies, Old and New Testament.

Bible guide

John Grayston, *Explorer's Guide to the Bible*, Scripture Union, 2008

Daily Bible reading

Scripture Union publishes a comprehensive range of daily Bible guides, both in print and in electronic formats:

Daily Bread: For people who want to explore, understand and enjoy the Bible as they apply it to everyday life. (Also available in a large print version.)

Encounter with God: A thoughtful, in-depth aproach to systematic Bible reading applied to contemporary living.

Closer to God: For people who long to hear God's voice and experience his love and power.

WordLive: an innovative online Bible experience for groups and individuals. Check it out at **www.wordlive.org**

SU publications are available from Christian bookshops, on the Internet or via mail order:
• www.scriptureunion.org.uk/shop
• email info@scriptureunion.org.uk
• phone: 01908 856006
• write to: SU Mail Order, PO Box 5148, Milton Keynes MLO, MK2 2YX, UK

Notes